Faith, Freedom and the First Thanksgiving

Copyright © 2023 by JSB Morse. All Rights Reserved. Printed in the United States of America.
Quotes were taken from William Bradford's "Of Plymouth Plantation: 1620-1647"

This book was produced by Libertas Kids, an imprint of Code Publishing, Austin, TX. LibertasKids.com
ISBN 978-1-60020-095-3

In the year 1620, a group of devout Christians known as the Puritans set sail from England on a ship called the Mayflower. They were seeking a new land where they could worship God in the way they believed was right. Among them was a man named William Bradford, a pious man who strongly believed in God's providence.

Before the Pilgrims left England, they agreed that they would all work together to build a new community in America. They would share everything they had to provide for the common good, just like the earliest Christians.

But when they arrived in America and settled in a place they called Plymouth, that communal system of labor didn't work as well as they had hoped. Even though everyone was supposed to share equally in the work and the food, some were motivated to work harder than others. As Bradford wrote, "The young men, who were most able and fit for labor and service, did not want to spend their time and strength working for other men's wives and children without any recompense." It was a harsh winter, and nearly half of them died from sickness and hunger. William Bradford was one of the lucky ones who survived and was elected as the second governor of Pymouth Colony.

The following spring, a Native American named Tisquantum, or Squanto, came to visit the Pilgrims. Squanto told the Pilgrims his amazing story. He had previously been taken from his home to be sold as a slave in Spain. There, some Franciscan friars had rescued him from captivity and brought him into the Christian faith. He later traveled to England and learned English before returning to his native land and joining the Pokanoket tribe.

Squanto showed the Pilgrims how to plant corn and other crops to grow better using fish as fertilizer. He also taught them how to catch fish in the nearby streams and where to gather nuts and berries.

Thanks to Squanto's help, the Pilgrims were able to grow enough food to survive. So, when the Mayflower was repaired and ready to sail back to England, most of the Pilgrims decided to stay in Plymouth. They knew that despite the hardships, if they trusted in God's providence, He would provide for them.

After their first harvest, the Pilgrims invited their Native American friends to join them for a feast, which is now considered the first Thanksgiving. Together they shared a meal of turkey, corn, and other foods from the harvest and gave thanks to God for His gifts.

But even as they feasted, Bradford knew that the colony was still struggling to produce enough food for themselves. They had hoped that Squanto's teachings would be enough to ensure their survival, but even with the knowledge of how to procure food, the communal system of labor held them back and stifled production.

After another brutal winter, Governor Bradford decided to make a change. He realized that the communal system of labor was not working and that they needed to try something different "that they might not still thus languish in misery."

Bradford called a meeting of the community and proposed a new idea. Instead of contributing everything they worked for to the common stock, he suggested that each family should be given their own piece of land to farm. They would be responsible for it and they would be able to keep whatever they produced and then trade the surplus.

Some Pilgrims were skeptical of this idea at first. They were worried that it would lead to even more conflict and inequality within the community. But William Bradford was confident that it was the right thing to do.

In the end, the Pilgrims decided to give it a try. They divided up the land and started working on their own farms. It was still hard work, but then, almost as if by miracle, something amazing happened. Everyone was more motivated to work when they knew that their efforts would directly benefit their own family. They worked harder and smarter, and they started to produce more food than ever before.

As Bradford wrote, "This had very good success, for it made all hands very industrious, so as much more corn was planted than otherwise would have been by any means the Governor . . . could use, and saved him a great deal of trouble, and gave far better content. The women now went willingly into the field, and took their little ones with them to set corn; which before would allege weakness and inability; whom to have compelled would have been thought great tyranny and oppression."

"Instead of famine now God gave them plenty," Bradford continued, "and the face of things was changed, to the rejoicing of the hearts of many, for which they blessed God.... Any general want or famine hath not been amongst them since to this day."

The Pilgrims' struggles and triumphs in Plymouth laid the foundation for the American spirit of hard work, determination, and trust in God's providence that continues to inspire us today. Through their example, we learn that faith and freedom are a recipe for prosperity in the New World.

The End

www.ingramcontent.com/pod-product-compliance
Lightning Source LLC
Chambersburg PA
CBHW041602070526
44586CB00003BA/61